97 POSITIONS OF THE HEART

97 POSITIONS OF THE HEART

Jaik Josephson

*Illustrations by
Erin Josephson-Laidlaw*

The
Muses'
Company

The Muses' Company Series Editor: Clarise Foster
Cover art by Erin Josephson-Laidlaw
Book design by Relish New Brand Experience Inc.
Author photo of Jaik Josephson by Brent Lott
Author photo of Erin Josephson-Laidlaw by Tim Raffey
Printed and bound in Canada on 100% post-consumer recycled paper.

We acknowledge the financial support of the Manitoba Arts Council and The Canada Council for the Arts for our publishing program.

LIBRARY AND ARCHIVES CANADA CATALOGUING IN PUBLICATION

Josephson, Jaik, 1960-
97 positions of the heart / Jaik Josephson; illustrations by Erin Josephson-Laidlaw.

Poems.
ISBN 978-1-897289-77-8

1. Smart, Elizabeth, 1913-1986—Poetry. I. Josephson-Laidlaw, Erin, 1987-
II. Title. III. Title: Ninety-seven positions of the heart.

PS8619.O8465N55 2012 C811'.6 C2012-902453-8

J. Gordon Shillingford Publishing
P.O. BOX 86, RPO Corydon Avenue, Winnipeg, MB Canada R3M 3S3

Acknowledgements

97 POSITIONS OF THE HEART was born out of a late night dinner conversation at a farm in Dorset, England in 2008. Four friends—a choreographer, two theatre devisers and a poet sipped wine and dreamed aloud about just how to come together in a creative pact. Conversation was driven by a longing to collaborate across art forms and countries. Random ideas were tossed about and held up for consensus. It was the pioneering life and writing of Elizabeth Smart that came to overshadow all the prospective subjects. Smart's story was an obvious fit. She had passion enough for each of our voices. The backdrop for her transformative life was rooted in both Canada and England. We agreed that she was an author most deserving of celebration. The initial research and development took place in 2010, a fringe performance entitled *Bash On Regardless* was mounted in 2011 and the final incarnation was developed and performed as the centre piece of Winnipeg's Contemporary Dancers (WCD) 2011-12 season and later at the Canada Dance Festival in Elizabeth's hometown, Ottawa. In the end, the telling of Elizabeth's life has grown and brought together a choreographer, a writer, a visual artist, a dramaturge, actors, musicians and of course WCD's staggeringly resplendent dancers. I would like to acknowledge the many collaborators and supporters that have contributed along the way. Thanks to the Winnipeg Arts Council and their New Creations Fund, Arts Council England, Manitoba Arts Council, Canada Council for the Arts, Winnipeg's Contemporary Dancers, Brent Lott, Naomi Cooke, Lisa Harrison, Michelle Walker, Debbie Patterson, Shirley Grierson, Tim Church, William Grierson, Lise McMillan, Kristin Haight, Johanna Riley, Sarah Roche, Mark Sawh Medrano, Emma Rose, Kayla Henry, Dean Cowieson, Norma Lachance, WCD's emerging company VERGE, The School of Contemporary Dancers, Kathy Fenton, James Botaitis, Kayla Jeanson, Lindsay Alford, Erin Josephson-Laidlaw, Wendy Josephson and Mandi Kujawa.

That was my life out there, frail, fluttering. No wonder we insulate ourselves from wonders. Poetry is like this, it is moving, terrible, vivid. Look the other way when you write, or you may faint.

Elizabeth Smart, *In The Meantime* [1]

Table of Contents

The harmonics of all music and the mathematics of suspension bridges
cannot equate the angle of this head as it leans to one side
under the summer of its own coronals… Oh My Canadian.

George Barker, *Diary of George Barker*[2]

Introduction

97 POSITIONS OF THE HEART probes the awakening inner world of Canadian writer Elizabeth Smart. This collection of poems celebrates Smart's intensely lived quest for self-actualization. Her rapturous life story unfolds against the backdrop of a bewildering childhood, a tumultuous romantic pairing with English writer, George Barker, the experience of motherhood and her pursuit of a literary language that dares to speak a truth about life in the social margins. Staring down the punishing expectations for women in the first half of the last century, Elizabeth side-stepped convention to demand a place in life's grand adventure. Born into a prominent family within an unpopulated and undeveloped new country, she shirked the burgeoning class system that sought to claim her. The stirrings of artistic self expression preoccupied her childhood but the Canadian literary lens had not yet begun to take shape. There was as of yet, no place for Elizabeth. Her urgent pursuit of a muse was fuelled by the need to loosen the grip of an over-controlling mother who intended to define and choreograph her future. Smart's determination to embrace her own experience was charted by an impractical roadmap that directed this bohemian unwed mother of four to devour life unbridled and without apology.

Elizabeth Smart is most recognized for having authored the critically acclaimed *By Grand Central Station I Sat Down and Wept* (1945), one of the most highly regarded pieces of poetic prose ever written. Following this momentous splash into the book world, she went on to take a thirty two year absence before adding a prosaic meditation, journals, poetry collections and a book on gardening to her literary catalogue. Elizabeth's writing remains largely uncategorized given her search to discover a new literary language to step beyond the established tenets of storytelling. While the poems in this collection do not attempt to mimic Smart's sensibility, they are similarly grounded in the use of metaphoric leaning. Each piece is informed by both her writing and biographical map. As the poetry was birthed within a larger performance project, the text is reflective of a dialogue emerging from a collaborative network that incorporates dance, music and visual art. Each creative thread has become a part of an interactive vehicle to more fully reveal Elizabeth's story. The resulting narrative is a conversation that is sometimes directed toward George, sometimes toward Elizabeth's mother, and at other times, seemingly, toward a wider waiting world.

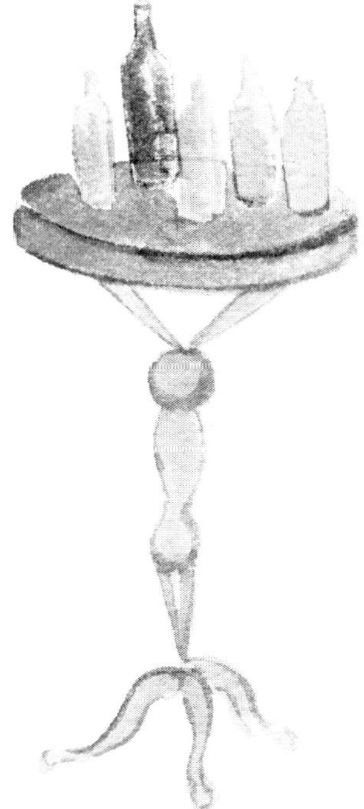

Death Announcement

It might have been ordinary.
Could have been a moment just like others.
But in the morning London haze of March 4th, 1986,
Elizabeth Smart let loose one final corporeal kick.
Her grown children carried on
unknowing in the dull dust of a Tuesday.
Sebastian slept late.
Georgina tidied dishes.
Christopher fussed with a knot of keys.
Didn't feel the exhale.
Didn't sense her brushing past the opening door.
Sebastian slept.
Georgina tidied.
And Christopher found the death.
Coffee cold beside her,
the body abandoned and upright in a chair, still clutched an earthly message.
'Christopher ring Eddie.'
Oh, so reassuring,
that tender looping line of blue.
It was no dictation just like others.
'Christopher ring Eddie,'
a last maternal beacon to 'carry on here, as I go.'
It might have been ordinary,
this ticket to finally begin.

Elizabeth left behind a blessed collection of siblings,
children,
grandchildren,
rascals,
plants and poems that she tended through her every day.
Among the bereaved are those who loved her two years
and those who loved her forty.
A tiny flicker sticks to them.
It was her hug designed to sweater through all manner of bullying weather.
Elizabeth—predeceased by parents, Russell and Louie Smart.
Elizabeth—predeceased by a youngest daughter,
Rose,
that most indomitable blossom of them all.

1913—Elizabeth Smart was born into an awkward Canada.
A country just learning to crawl.
Her father successful.
A mother renowned.
The Smarts lived Ottawa-cosy
—summered on Kingsmere Lake.
Childhood journals confirm
that arms of aspen welcomed Betty
into a secret that would whisper wild throughout her days.
It was here,
mooning in an assemblage of maples,
that her lifelong conversation with the cosmos was awoken.

Poems began as a girl.
It was the way life called to her.
Though groomed to be the butterfly,
some prized wife,
an opinionless hostess
—despite all ceremony,
the cotillions,
private schools,
piano study
—Elizabeth was forever impatient to burst life.
She made off into a great world from which she plucked her George.
Thunder came sudden,
and there would sometimes be an 'us' in magnificent bodies, words and babies.
Sometimes an 'us',
but George could not be a well washed husband.
Elizabeth repositioned, yearning for her own poetry.
Her own light.
It might have all been ordinary.
Could have been a moment just like others
but it was not.

Bewilderness

Mother,
she's a hollering downpour.
Oversees a collection of people.
Orchestrates the who's-who.
She's perfected the luncheon.
Has a family that fits into her guest list,
the menu,
the seating,
a husband successful,
daughters in-training and a baby will carry the name.
'Sit quiet now, Betty,'
Has her hands full.
'Just wait,'
for after the gossip and cake.
'Wait,'
first she shouts at the cook.
And I,
an invisible child,
unseen behind her insistence of fog,
just slip away.
Blossom wild inside a forest,

where my name is whispered.
An articulate blessing
from this custodial hover of trees.

But
Mother,
she's a mighty rumble.
Thunders 'NO'.
We are children with too much engine.
Threatens to scrape the gypsy out of us.
Says how we make her
tear at my dress with a claw.
Squash me and push where I cannot fit.
She stops sudden.
Sees fingers and blood.
Hugs-sorry for what she had to do
but
it's from an assemblage of maples,
that I am held.
Luminous,
forgiven,
an almost escape.

Yet she baits.
Beckons home with mother-kisses.
Sunshine for now.
Baptizes three girls with a trickery of light.
We are noticed
in offerings of currant cakes and pretend,
dress up,
giggling,
hats of feather and pink meringue.
If I might
fasten to afternoon kindness,
ride through flux and hard fall.
If I could
only love her
enough
but
jollities are soon pulled by the root.

Mother
makes shade now.
He's a nestling protected.
Born with a career path.
My unbothered brother,
naps plump behind curtain.
Sleeps ornamental.
Doesn't rouse to storms.

He still knows mommy-love in a basket
while unseen girls empty ashtrays.
Fluent in polish and curtsy,
these daughters of the capital,
given up to a regimen of finishing touch.
Still,
I reach out for what's igneous.
Confirm an existence in Precambrian secret.
Study
just how juniper finds cracks to demand
life.

Mother
calls me into unpredictable weather.
She is wind pushing back.
Blusters a wall
and banished sisters don't dare on a porch.
Girls, bewildered,
sit tallest to shortest,
for now.
Unaware of the possibilities of flight,
yet knowing
we must not show plumage.
Disguise all this ripening.
Hide the bastard wing.
Our awkward bloom in rabbit coats.

Three
in mauve skirts
and matching stomachs turned stone.
While mother shoves air.
Mutters
'you don't let me be pillow.'
Curses my mooning in the woods.
Together
we endure this tempest.
Watch for 5:30.
Await a buick in the drive.
Father,
our hope for democracy.
A chinook to waft warm
or maybe just notice.
Maybe,
but for now,
oh benevolent balsam,
outstretched arms of aspen,
launch your sparrows skyward.
Together
and beyond.

The Welcoming Guts

I'm begun.
In these sloshing guts of Siboney,
my rescuing ship begun.
Made new
in a jostling hegira.
At last to ride a lumpy ocean,
away from her gaze that anchors.
I am finally seen
inside a great dreamed boat.

Oh, top deck is politesse,
the champagne and bon voyage,
but I'm unmopped below.
Crammed
where third class stomachs splash a hideous glisten,
these loud smelling mud-smudged strangers
and what they are gets in my goddamned hair.
So prurient.
So forbidden
by mother's pot of hate.

I'm begun
but haven't yet their language.
I don't know these foreign words for mercy.
Can't surrender to pitch and yaw
though I too have risen from some dust of long, long waiting.
I too,
am made exile
—spat out
from the bullying mouth of appetite
and war
and weather.
Know atrocity's grinding chew
but my own hunger,
still,
it's not convincing.

Such an unlikely seafarer.
I've arrived in a whimsical dress,
the last brash vestige,
a camouflage to belonging.
Too young and Canada,
I'm big land awaiting poets.
Empty and without decay,
I must
pull out these moonstone buttons
—must

rip at cerulean blue chiffon.
See the stink of me?
The bend in unison,
the jerk and then correct.
Do I wear their yellow scars?
Is it seen in me,
that glow behind my broken windows?

Still mother interrupts.
Throws her net of sobs.
She insists on detours from a room inside my dream.
Threatens to snap her own head off
if I don't obey.
But some tousled traveller sees,
he offers a palsied reach,
holds out his dented cup
and whispers a Polish prayer.
He strokes my hair like benediction
and I drink of a vulgar soup.
Sip this broth of tears and armpit
to cascade warm and christen
what is me
inside.

It's true.
I can stand up to the murderous act.
I'll not be pulled back guilty.
Not
be stolen from life inevitable.
Yes, love accepts like nature
and those cast out see those cast out.
Our great predicament recognized.
Oh, begin me,
for I've not been so unrehearsed.
Never
this thoroughly unlaced
—my every cell so plump with proclamation.
Pulse of a blessed vessel,
I've glimpsed holy.
Been let in on religion.
I am citizen of the human body.
Finally one
with these wave battered gutter pups.
I'm a refugee here upon the water,
inside
the gestating guts of Siboney.
We sway comely,
vomit,
cling and slosh.

We share our dirty bread,
sing these rascal shanties,
for hymns do sail us
to our home,
brand new.

George Enters

Oh, welcome you generous smash of long-waited-for lightning.
Thank you, dear thunder in London,
when freedom came so sudden,
So violent.
HE has entered the room
just as I thought I might die by the hand of Canadian boredom.
Welcome the blessed shine of it all.
Poetry lives unexpected in the dull dust of Tuesday!
Mother, HE is finally here.
I've been watching for this knee-buckling bang.
Breath-caged blue and waiting to burst life.
Until now,
mindless mostly,
a tedium relentless,
this drab forever-drumming through my slow collection of minutes.
Thank you, dear rescuing night, for your door.
I am ready to be written in stars.
Life calls in new language.
Words spoken only by me and some George—
an 'us' I don't know but somehow
strangely

expected
do know.
George?
Complete me, my thunder clap.
Find me in your juicy sounds.
Let bubbles run warm over words.
Mother—on page 32,
George entered the room today
calling
'Can you hear me my honied dove?'
HE asks 'Can you make a song of my voice?'
And I say 'Yes. Please dream of hurricanes to come and stir these waters where I swim.'
It is time.
Mother,
I scream pain under your kitchen window.
Curtains of linen hung
to hold close your ignorance of what has finally crashed into the world.
You see?
We reached into midnight for that moon which must be born
and I can't go back to "old clothes and porridge."[3]
I won't.
I am ready for a teetering walk in the dark
on those highest of heels.
I am ready for that merciful car.
Ready to ride
to where suckling jazz wails feral,

to where my people smoke and laugh absurd in their feathers and uncaring.
The waiting's over.
'Mother may I go now?'
Mother 'may I take my ticket and begin?'

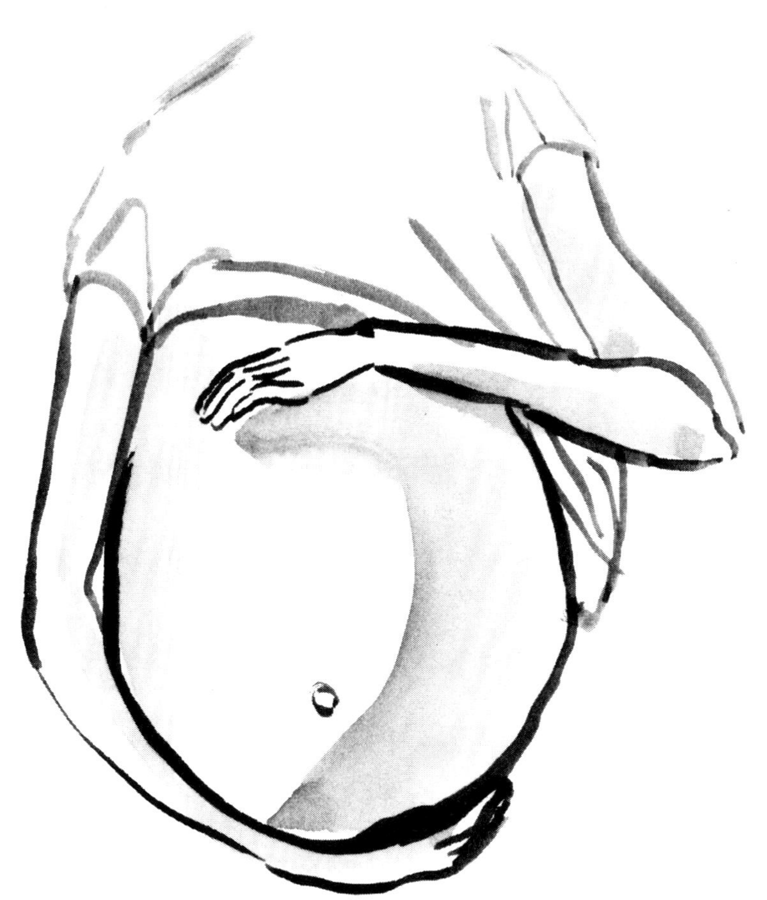

Pender Harbour

She insists,
'awake!'
Water-bash-star,
'awake!'
My impatient thunder readies,
unapologetic.
Tries to be known from a swollen place.
Announces herself with this kick inside,
this push,
shoreward where fishermen slumber.
Out there,
a village lulled by slap and spray.
It's not the haughty sleep of Ottawa,
'awake!'
Oh, little weald without curtsy,
so not sorry for your dawdle in the woods.
Oh, salty place,
surrendered to curl
and dissolve.
The reach across long miles of barren mattress,
I take what tide will offer.
Elbow prop on sleepy banks,
my lonesome scan
of a cabin-dark tick-tick water-glass found-feather night-stand unopened-mother-letter
sewing-basket pencil almost-poem ashtray empty-bedside-chair,
'awake!'

Again positions
—demands to be written,
and no one sits smoking in a usual beige sweater.
No man to watch this round woman rub whispers into the lump of love's reward.
George has left.
He's gone
again
but
I'll put my own kettle on.
I've found my gentle Pender.
Become velvet,
a soon-to-be mother watching winds hush,
waiting in gravity's coax,
I abide
here.
This little spot on earth is mine.
Here,
a beautiful bastard alive
insists inside me.
Wild and lapping
at two in a buttoned up morning.
Sweatered swell-belly by a breath of window,
waddle careful,
"slow"
for there's a flood afoot.
And old wood groans baritone.
Yearns to spark life in a creak

It's how nature pushes.
Kicks for more room,
the little insist,
her almost-growl,
her nudge and settle
again
'awake!'
We do this.
No, I won't be afraid
—not scared of blood and water rising.
Women, we churn
and do hope.
Women,
we rip.
It's how nature makes room for what's new,
what's been long imagined.
Here,
a snug harbour,
wished
on the ceiling of a childhood bedroom.
Memorized
in measured breaths of ocean,
finally.
'Awake!'
Women, we do this.
Just as poetry promised,
I turn out the lamp and write by my own light.

Birth Announcement — By Grand Central Station

On November 9th of 1941,
following a sometimes perilous ocean voyage,
By Grand Central Station I Sat Down and Wept
ripped its way from a place
cold of climate
and into the arms of an eager and unholy tribe.
It weighed in at a full 128 pages
once rinsed of the frost
and asking permission.

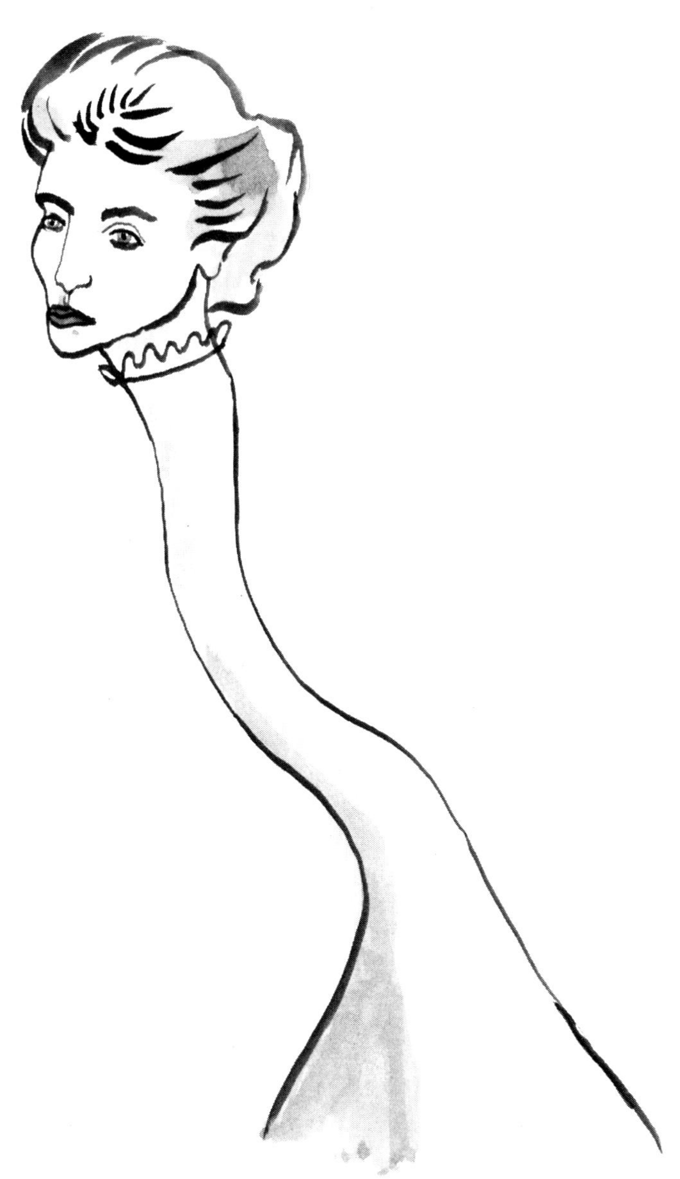

Dear Betty

My dearest Betty:

Is it a bad dream or is this what has come of your choices? I have now finished your book and this marks my eleventh fretful attempt to put words to paper. It seems I can't avoid being hurtful. Surely you realize that no mother could be exposed in such an unflattering portrayal without being bruised. Despite occasional moments of beauty, I must side with the critic from *The New Statesman* who describes your poetic carrying on as some 20 years out of date. The same is said of George but perhaps I do not understand literature. All in all, I'm just grateful that your father is not alive to know the shame of your having published such flagrant eroticism. He sacrificed everything for us. And for that you gave him sorrow and stomach ulcers. It is with a broken heart that I burned my copy of *By Grand Central Station I Sat Down and Wept*. On learning that there were six more for sale at Murphy-Gambles, I rushed to buy and burn those also. These things I do in the interest of thwarting any further humiliation to the Smart family. You need not worry, Elizabeth. I have been in touch with an understanding friend at External Affairs to ensure no further copies need make their way to Canada.

I won't say more, but despite your vagabond existence I have never stopped loving you and intend to increase your dress allowance to $125 a month.

With deepest love,
Mummy [4]

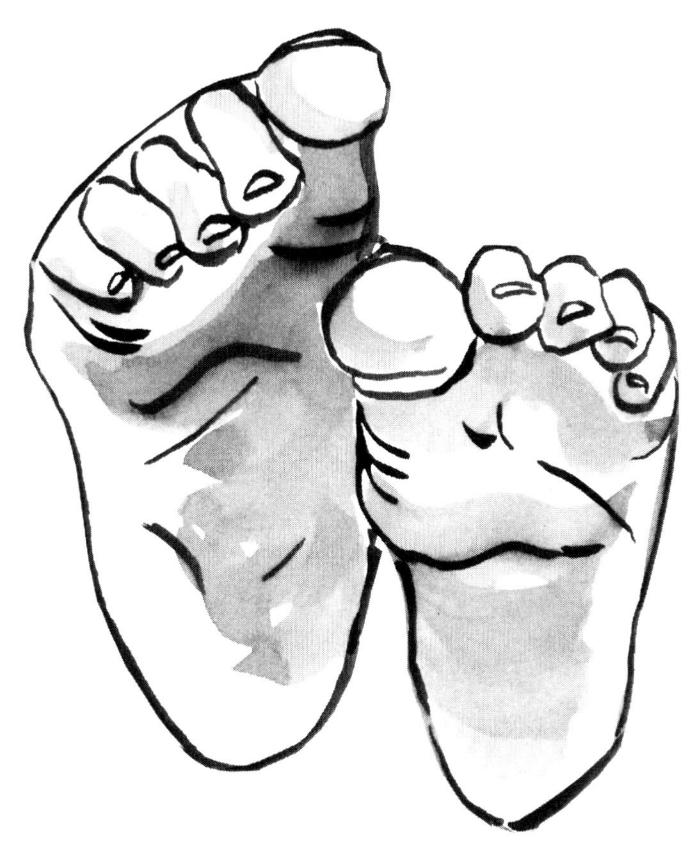

Birth Announcement — Big-toed Christopher

On July 23rd of 1943,
following a sometimes perilous ocean voyage,
one big-toed Christopher Barker
ripped his way from a vagina
and into the arms of an eager and unholy family.
He weighed in at a full ten pounds
once rinsed of the salt and seaweed.
Christopher weathered unthinkable prenatal adventures
including the untimely separation of his parents;
the 35 pound weight of his frightened sister sitting on him in a wartime torpedo-struck ship to England,
a two day interrogation at the British Ministry of Information,
delousing,
homelessness,
rations,
air-raids,
and a most welcomed reunion with his father.
It is his mother's deepest wish that his bastard status keep him unburdened by "the bores,
the snobs,
those petty
and afraid."[5]
She reminds him that it was Scarlatti that he hummed to from the womb
and, though hearts surely break,
he need not discard a belief in songs and stars
and books
and just how truest midnight shines in both men and women.

Christopher has been designed by poets to climb and sing
and not ever fear his great gift
of love.

Upon the 5th week anniversary of his arrival,
twins
Anthony and Anastasia
were born to Christopher's father and stepmother,
Jessica.[6]

Begging and Awful

Begging and awful in an all night diner.
I'm just awful,
while Pity sleeps her innocent sleep.
Dreams those mousey wishes that melt your resolve to be
free.
She steals from truth.
Sleeps,
unknowing how you tiptoe away
to a late night breakfast.
Are you listening?
I hate the waitress.
Fuck her.
Once proud daisy tires behind an ear.
Stupid.
Fuck.
All smiles
and struts fake for some 25,
maybe 50
extra
greasy cents
while we don't talk about what happened to the size of love.
Are you listening?
I'm here.
A ranting enemy,
can't pity Pity.

Spitting curses at reckless lust.
I'm here
but you've turned away.
Here,
a spectacle of truth ignored.
I'll not be made the dullard
pleading into a wandering eye.
Are you really thinking about fucking that waitress?
Bite a freckled shoulder
and her ridiculous yellow uniform falls to the cafe floor.
Push yourself inside her tawdry hole
and away from me,
begging and awful in a vinyl booth.
Love dismissed and Pity picked.
How is it that I've arrived here?
Left pleading over bacon, eggs and heartbreak in a snuck moment?
Remember
the giggles
last night,
hollering our electric song.
Remember,
I'm the one you plucked from a great grey world.
Just as I
chose
you

for a conversation of ancient words,
modern ideas.

Us,
chain-smoking in a motel bed.
Remember,
I plucked you from a poem of the world.
Chose you to be the one who feeds me apples.
Last night,
I thought you understood
how a truth about love is absolute
—bigger than the three of us.
Our love,
I thought you knew the magnitude
but you've arrived at midnight wearing guilty lies and whispers.
Somehow,
I've become the other
left to hate the cluck of an idiot waitress.
Made to be enemy of an unknowing wife.
It is me,
accepting the refill,
sleepless and swollen
—purple behind dark glasses.
It is heavy without you but I'll carry our love.
Fuck.

This coffee is tepid,
toast indistinct.
But I try to slow time in these coffee shop shadows.
Hold on to all possible lingering
before your tiptoe back
to such pitiable duty.

ALL
NIGHT

The Worm-kissers

Four by tumbling heat,
each deliberately written.
Four little worm-kissers wanted,
each,
a seed inside our story.
Georgina, Christopher, Sebastian, Rose
—one by shimmering one.
Stake place within my meadow.
Georgina, Christopher, Sebastian, Rose
—swim empyrean inside my sea.
Georgina, Christopher, Sebastian
—deliver and release
into our family forest.

The Colonic

Tonight,
I make my way
out from under burden,
away from predictable days.
Tonight,
I'm going up.
Sweet rain and moon conspire
—cast a midnight shine.
Glisten the black brick of Dean Street.
Ring Cunty's bell
and reach for the big drink.
Up,
up the dirty stairs,
in search of smoke and gorgeous mischief.
Slow welcoming whining door
reveals
the open legs of Soho,
spectacular!
From under a towering velvet turban
Miss Mother Molly Parkin smokes on a bar stool
—calls out her usual 'Piss off, ya boring cunt.'
I enter the little miracle room,
womb walls of vomitous green.
The Colonic,
where everyone talks to everyone.
All of us outsiders,

inside.
Misfits here,
where the pissheads get arseholed every single night
and I drink
and I sing
and I fight myself into existence.
I'm up for the big drink.
Here for the whiskey oiled words.
To feed on angular poems,
out loud,
by heart.
And all the while Campy Ida pours more drinks.
Love and rudeness by the glassful,
couldn't care how the ashtrays are always full.
She's here to enforce the golden rule:
'JUST DON'T BE FUCKING DULL' here,
at 41 Dean Street.
Here,
sex hangs in the air.
Like jazz it demands truth's attention.
Muriel, the grand proprietor,
Muriel, the benevolent witch,
the nanny of us all
dispensing her rude warm milk around a barely stand up piano
says
'You don't have to be "a drunk, a black, a homosexual or battered love object"[7]

to sing our song of bliss, bliss, bliss but at The Colonic … it surely helps.'
Trannie Frances postures her poison pink
"Did ya ever see a nose like that?"[8]
Here,
in these corners of dim lit minds,
Carmel yells back butch
"Are you talking about her fucking ass or her face?"[9]
And there's this chorus of gravel laughter,
here in the arms of night.
But not to be outdone,
some angry bilious dandy
yells throaty
"She's had more pricks than you've had hot dinners."[10]
And I know
I belong
at The Colonic,
where our rascal choir brays songs of monstrosity and heart.
It's from inside such horrible harmony
that I forget
all that trouble with mothers.
Don't notice the shame,
those letters from Canada,
the forever not measuring up.
I forget the appetites teaming,
trouble with lovers,
his hunger for my dress allowance,

demands and bruising.
I forget
that problem with children.
Four open mouths
baby birdcall for bus fare and lunches.
Yeah.
I gotta get home
but Muriel delivers one final kindly gentle gin,
whispers 'Closing time'
but I'm all
'Just keep Cass away from me' as London's sun comes up.
Guess I'm almost done.
'Keep her away.'
And it's closing time.
Ida sweeps,
sweeps
the slow loving George Barker glitter
from the morning Colonic floor.

Celestial Navigation

Do not reach to anchor.
This midnight moon is but a rest stop.
Mustn't grip for permanence.
You're not some slippered husband,
not that gentle father reading,
no child upon each knee.
It's just tonight.
Tonight I offer arms
to bandage 'round a battered traveller's heart.
Take these just-for-now arms
that cradle,
that hand-feed apple slices
and rock
you muttering silly in the dark.

Tonight
we sip whiskey and remember.
"Remember?"
No sound had been so reassuring.
That pop
and tear-smudged hiss,
a first time
listening.
Oh, Scarlatti on the Wurlitzer
—yeah,

we played it again
and again,
again.

"Remember?"
No kiss so reassuring,
driving reckless in America,
that ebb,
the flow.
Fast curves in California,
pulling over
a first giggling time.
Oh, midnight fuck in the back of an unreliable Ford
—yeah,
we played it again
and again,
again.

"Remember?"
For just tonight
cuz it's not me you call acushla.
These sleeping children
are not the beating of your heart.
We do not seek to moor you.
Remember

it's Cass that made this bruise.
Cass who left this sliver where you love.
It's not our long pull of lust that has you beg for marriage.
Do not confuse Scarlatti with some rescue.
These arms,
most temporary
arms,
just-for-now.
I've long ago stopped late night hand-wringing,
snuffed out all bitter wait,
emptied bedside drawers of lying poems that promise,
understood who I am among many.
Those women,
the men
who play again and again,
again.
In your "crowded bed"[11] I know who I am.
Learned not to need a man
or woman.
Learned to make love with the long fingers of my own poetry.

George,
do not look back wriggling,
hooked by regret.
Move along steady, old friend.
Move free,

unwounded,
while our sons and daughters sleep halcyon under eiderdown.
"Trust"
they dream turquoise dreams,
birthday horses
—"no! shhh.
You'll not burden babies untroubled by absence.
You'll not!"
There are so many fathers to bring home,
luggage brimmed with masculine need and instruction.
Not to worry.
Our children learned well to carry longing.
I taught them.
It's a poet that they need
for there are just so many fathers.

All I ask is simple.
When next you meet some years from now
there'll be questions across a supper table.
Do explain our love was true
and point them to Parnassus.
George,
never to be father.
Not to be husband,
though tonight these arms shall cradle.
Rock

you upward,
up and brave
toward departure.
Remember
fix all inquiry on the sky.
Don't look back.
Do not wonder.
Don't mistake my candlelit window for the moon
for we have tried these "97 positions of the heart."[12]
Surely,
We've mouthed radiance
until all hurt resumed.
We've tried
to saddle aches
again and again,
again,
such incessant transfer of the weight.
Love leans
but cramps again
—settles to pinch once more.
"Remember?"
All this dog-eared toss and turn.
We just couldn't find comfortable.
And you must let not
my tiny flicker be your compass.
It's just a fragile flame.

A little fire just-for-now,
to guide remembering
—a light not meant to complicate your way.

Once Wild

A bird once wild,
returns
red-winged
and looking for the moment
four babies ago
when a sky was more a sky.

A mother once wild,
captured,
bound to
unthinkable casualty
of amnion tear,
abides this weeping shadow.

Oh, woman once wild,
unfold,
go deep
into a forest quiet
enough to listen
and remember your own voice.

Endnotes

1. Elizabeth Smart, *In The Meantime* (Ottawa: Deneau Publishers, 1984) 51.
2. George Barker, *Diary of George Barker* (National Library of Canada: Box 62, F2) qtd. in Rosemary Sullivan, *By Heart* (Toronto: Penguin Books, 1992) 155.
3. Kim Echlin, *Elizabeth Smart: A Fugue Essay on Women and Creativity* (Toronto: Women's Press, 2004) 222.
4. The poem "Dear Betty" was inspired by a letter from Louie Smart, 14, June 1946. National Library of Canada: Box 15, F3.
5. Elizabeth Smart, *Autobiographies*, ed. Christina Burridge (Vancouver: William Hoffer/Tanks, 1987) 44.
6. The poem "Birth Announcement—Big-toed Christopher" was inspired by Elizabeths's journal writing found in *Autobiographies*, ed. Christina Burridge. Vancouver: William Hoffer/Tanks, 1987.
7. Kim Echlin, *Elizabeth Smart: A Fugue Essay on Women and Creativity* (Toronto: Women's Press, 2004) 164.
8. Ibid. 162.
9. Ibid.
10. Elizabeth Smart, *Muriel* (National Library of Canada: Box 55, F25) qtd. in Rosemary Sullivan, *By Heart* (Toronto: Penguin Books, 1992) 249.
11. Elizabeth Smart, *Letter to George Barker* (National Library of Canada: Box 15, F3) qtd. in Rosemary Sullivan, *By Heart* (Toronto: Penguin Books, 1992) 234.
12. Elizabeth Smart, *Preliminary Notes* (National Library of Canada: Box 51, F2) qtd. in Rosemary Sullivan, *By Heart* (Toronto: Penguin Books, 1992) 330.